FAWN WEAVER

THE LIFE FROM
BEGINNING TO THE END

BY FACT PUBLISHER

TABLE OF CONTENT

INTRODUCTION

THE UNLIKELY ENTREPRENEUR

Prior to Uncle Nearest Whiskey, Fawn Weaver's life was very different from the world of spirits and entrepreneurship. Fawn was born and raised in California, where her family valued education and hard work.

Her parents, both high school sweethearts, instilled in her a strong spirit of determination and perseverance. Fawn's early years were characterised by a love of learning, and she excelled in school, earning high grades and developing a strong interest in history and literature.

As a teenager, Fawn's creative side began to show. She discovered a passion for writing, pouring her heart and soul into poems and short stories. Her writing became an escape, a means of expressing herself and processing the world around her.

Fawn's parents recognized her talent and encouraged her to pursue a career in writing.

She went on to study English literature in college, where she honed her skills and gained a deep appreciation for the power of language.

Following college, Fawn's life took an unexpected turn. She got a job in the technology industry as a marketing specialist for a small startup. The fast-paced world of technology was far from the literary circles she had once imagined, but Fawn thrived in it. She quickly established herself as an effective communicator, able to distil complex ideas into compelling narratives. Her writing abilities, which were previously reserved for creative pursuits, became a valuable asset in the business world.

As Fawn moved up the corporate ladder, she began to feel unfulfilled. The tech industry, while profitable, lacked the sense of purpose she had found in writing. She felt like a cog in a machine, producing marketing copy with no real sense of passion or purpose.

Fawn's creative spark, once a blazing flame, had dimmed to a faint flicker.

During this period of disillusionment, Fawn came across the story of Nathan "Nearest" Green, a former slave who became the first African American master distiller in the US. Fawn was captivated by Nearest's story, drawn to the similarities between his journey and hers.

Fawn, like Nearest, had faced her own set of challenges, including navigating the male-dominated tech industry and figuring out where she fit in the world. As she learned more about Nearest's history, Fawn felt a sense of purpose that she had been missing.

Fawn's life changed dramatically when she discovered Nearest's story. She began to see the world in a new light, realising the potential of entrepreneurship to effect positive change. Fawn's passion for writing, which was previously reserved for creative pursuits, was reignited. She began writing about Nearest, putting her heart and soul into the story. The more she wrote, the more she realised that Nearest's legacy deserved to be shared with the world.

Others were sceptical of Fawn's decision to leave the tech industry and pursue a career in whiskey. Friends and family questioned her sanity, asking why she would leave a lucrative career to pursue a dream. But Fawn remained undeterred. She saw an opportunity to honour Nearest's legacy by launching a brand that would recognize the whiskey industry's unsung heroes.

As Fawn began her journey, she encountered a steep learning curve. She knew nothing about whiskey, much less the complexities of distillation and production. She was determined to learn, so she poured over books and sought out industry mentors. Fawn's writing skills, which were previously reserved for marketing copy, were now focused on creating a brand narrative that would appeal to whiskey enthusiasts.

The early days of Uncle Nearest Whiskey were marked by hardship and perseverance. Fawn encountered rejection and scepticism at every turn, from investors who doubted her ability to succeed in a male-dominated industry to whiskey connoisseurs who questioned her lack of experience. But Fawn wouldn't give up. She found strength in Nearest's story, reminding herself that the former slave had overcome far greater challenges to achieve his goals.

As Uncle Nearest Whiskey took shape, Fawn's enthusiasm and dedication began to pay off. The brand gained traction as whiskey enthusiasts and industry insiders became aware of its unique story. Fawn's writing, which had once been a source of creative expression, had evolved into a powerful tool for creating a brand that would transform the whiskey industry.

Fawn Weaver's unlikely journey from technology marketer to whiskey entrepreneur demonstrated the power of passion and perseverance. Her story serves as a reminder that success is not solely determined by experience or background, but by a willingness to take risks and pursue one's dreams, no matter how impossible they may appear.

CHAPTER 1

GROWING UP FAWN

Fawn Weaver's childhood was a tapestry of love, laughter, and education. She was born into a close-knit family in California and was the pride of her parents. Her father, a hardworking man with a golden heart, instilled in her strong values and morals. Her mother, a free spirit with a creative streak, fostered Fawn's imagination and passion for the arts. They worked together to create a warm and welcoming home in which Fawn felt comfortable exploring and expressing herself.

Growing up, Fawn was an inquisitive and adventurous child. She spent hours playing in the backyard with her siblings, creating fantastical worlds and making up stories that transported her to faraway lands. Her parents recognized her creativity and encouraged her to pursue her interests, whether it was writing, drawing, or dancing.

Fawn's childhood was one of wonder, when everything seemed possible and her imagination was limitless.

Fawn's family served as her rock, support system, and guiding light. Her parents, despite not being wealthy, worked hard to provide for their children, instilling in them a strong work ethic and a sense of responsibility. Despite their differences, Fawn's siblings were her closest friends, partners in crime, and confidants. They navigated the ups and downs of childhood together, sharing laughter, tears, and lifelong memories.

Fawn's grandmother, a feisty and independent woman who survived the Great Depression, was one of her earliest influences. Her grandmother's stories of resilience, perseverance, and determination left an indelible impression on Fawn's young mind. She admired her grandmother's strength and courage, as well as her sense of purpose, which motivated her to make a difference in the world.

Fawn's love of learning was fostered by her parents, who encouraged her to read widely and pursue her interests. She devoured books of all genres, from fantasy to history, and developed a lifelong passion for writing. Her parents recognized her talent and encouraged her creativity, providing her with the tools and resources she needed to perfect her craft.

As Fawn grew into adolescence, she began to develop her own style and identity. She was drawn to the arts, especially music and literature, and would spend hours listening to her favourite bands and reading her favourite authors. Fawn's parents supported her despite their lack of understanding of her preferences, recognizing that her uniqueness was a strength rather than a weakness.

Fawn's early influences were diverse and wide-ranging. She was drawn to strong, independent women who had left their mark on the world, from Frida Kahlo to Maya Angelou. She saw in them a sense of purpose, drive, and determination that encouraged her to pursue her own goals. Fawn's parents, while not perfect, instilled in her a sense of self-worth, confidence, and possibility that she would carry with her for the rest of her life.

As Fawn reflected on her childhood, she realised that her family, early influences, and her own sense of curiosity had all shaped her personality. She was a creator, a dreamer, and a doer, motivated by a sense of purpose and a desire to make a difference in the world. Fawn's childhood may not have been perfect, but it was hers, and it provided her with the tools, confidence, and courage to pursue her dreams, no matter how impossible they appeared.

Fawn Weaver's childhood exemplified the power of love, family, and early influences. It was a reminder that our childhood experiences shape, mould, and inspire us to become the people we are meant to be. Fawn's story is a beacon of hope, a reminder that with hard work, determination, and a sense of purpose, we can overcome any challenge, achieve our goals, and leave a lasting impact on the world.

CHAPTER 2

REBEL WITHOUT A CAUSE

Fawn's teenage years were turbulent, filled with rebellion, experimentation, and a search for identity. She was a creative, free-spirited, and nonconformist who was constantly challenging the status quo and pushing boundaries. Her parents, while loving and supportive, frequently found themselves at odds with their daughter's antics, struggling to strike a balance between their desire to give her freedom and their need to protect her.

One of Fawn's earliest rebellious phases was her interest in the punk rock scene. She was drawn to the music's energy, raw emotion, and anti-establishment message. Fawn spent hours listening to bands like The Clash, The Sex Pistols, and Black Flag, feeling a connection with their DIY spirit and rejection of mainstream values. She began to go to punk rock concerts, frequently sneaking out of the house to catch a show at a local club or warehouse.

Fawn's parents, while they didn't understand her passion for punk rock, recognized it as a phase, a way for her to express herself and assert her independence. They gave her the freedom to pursue her interests, as long as she did not jeopardise her safety or education. Fawn's rebellion was not about causing chaos or destruction; it was about discovering her own voice, style, and sense of purpose.

As Fawn progressed through her adolescence, she developed an interest in writing. She had always been a creative person, but now she was determined to improve her craft and become a writer who could make a difference. Fawn spent hours writing poetry, short stories, and essays, putting her heart and soul into her work. She devoured books by her favourite authors, including Kerouac and Hemingway, and began to develop her own distinct voice, one that was raw, honest, and unapologetic.

One significant event that shaped Fawn's adolescence was her decision to take a gap year after high school. She had always felt like she didn't fit into the traditional mould, and that she needed time to pursue her interests and forge her own path. Fawn's parents were initially hesitant, but eventually supported her decision, recognizing that it was an opportunity for her to grow, learn, and discover her own sense of purpose.

Fawn spent her gap year exploring and discovering herself. She travelled, volunteered, and worked odd jobs, always looking for new opportunities and challenges. Fawn travelled throughout Europe, backpacking through France and Italy, as well as Africa, where she volunteered at a wildlife sanctuary. She worked as a waitress, bartender, and freelance writer, constantly looking for new opportunities and adventures.

Fawn reflected on her teenage years, realising that they had been a time of growth, experimentation, and self-discovery. She was a rebel, a nonconformist, and a free spirit who was constantly challenging the status quo and pushing the envelope. Fawn's teenage years had been chaotic and uncertain, but they were also a time of great creativity, passion, and purpose.

Fawn Weaver's teenage years demonstrated the power of rebellion, self-discovery, and significant events. They served as a reminder that our adolescence is a time of growth, exploration, and self-discovery, when we have the ability to shape our own destiny and forge our own path. Fawn's story is a beacon of hope, demonstrating that with courage, determination, and a sense of purpose, we can overcome any obstacle, achieve our goals, and leave a lasting impact on the world.

CHAPTER 3

THE BIRTH OF UNCLE NEAREST

Fawn Weaver's passion for whiskey was not a sudden epiphany, but rather a gradual discovery, beginning with a chance encounter and culminating in a brand that would make history. It was a journey that would take her from technology to whiskey, from California to Tennessee, and from uncertainty to purpose.

Uncle Nearest's story began with a visit to a local whiskey distillery in Tennessee. Fawn, who had always been fascinated by the world of spirits, had decided to take a tour of the distillery in the hopes of learning more about the whiskey-making process.

As she walked through the facility, she was struck by the rich history and tradition all around her. She saw the old stills, the wooden barrels, and the rows of bottles, each filled with a liquid that seemed to tell its own story.

While touring the distillery, Fawn met the master distiller, a man with a friendly demeanour and a wealth of knowledge. He explained the art of whiskey-making to her, emphasising the importance of grain, water, and wood, as well as the patience and dedication required to produce fine whiskey. Fawn was captivated by his enthusiasm, expertise, and love of the craft. She saw in him a kindred spirit, someone motivated by a desire to create something truly exceptional.

Fawn left the distillery with a sense of excitement and possibility. She'd found a new passion, interest, and sense of purpose. She began reading everything she could about whiskey, from books on the history of whiskey production to articles on the latest trends and innovations. She attended whiskey tastings, festivals, and workshops, always looking for new knowledge and experiences.

Fawn's passion for whiskey quickly evolved into a business idea. She saw an opportunity to create a brand that would celebrate whiskey's rich history and tradition, as well as honour the masters who had come before her. She began to develop a concept for a brand called Uncle Nearest Premium Whiskey, which would honour the first African American master distiller in the United States.

Fawn faced numerous challenges while developing her brand, including finding the right distillery and perfecting her recipe. She worked tirelessly, dedicating her heart and soul to every aspect of the brand, from label design to marketing strategy. She visited Tennessee, Kentucky, and other whiskey-producing states, meeting with distillers, blenders, and other industry professionals.

Fawn's hard work and dedication quickly paid off. Uncle Nearest Premium Whiskey debuted to critical acclaim, with whiskey enthusiasts and industry insiders praising its smooth, rich flavour and historical significance. The brand quickly developed a devoted following, with fans from all over the world seeking out Fawn's whiskey.

As Fawn reflected on her journey, she realised that the birth of Uncle Nearest had been a watershed moment in her life. It gave her a sense of purpose, direction, and fulfilment. She had created something truly exceptional, a brand that would have a long-term impact on the whiskey industry.

Fawn Weaver's story demonstrates that passion, dedication, and hard work can lead to greatness. It is a testament to the power of entrepreneurship, innovation, and pursuing one's dreams. Uncle Nearest Premium Whiskey is more than a brand; it represents what can be accomplished when we combine our passions, talents, and values.

CHAPTER 4

BREAKING BARRIERS

Fawn Weaver's journey in the whiskey industry was not without challenges. As a black woman, she faced challenges that her male peers did not. She was frequently the only woman in the room, the only person of colour, and the only one with a unique viewpoint. However, Fawn was not deterred by obstacles. She was motivated by a love of whiskey, a desire to succeed, and a refusal to be limited by the status quo.

Fawn's biggest challenge was a lack of representation in the industry. She was frequently the only woman at whiskey tastings, festivals, and workshops. She was frequently the only person of colour in an otherwise all-white crowd.

However, Fawn did not let this intimidate her. Instead, she saw it as a chance to make a difference, to bring a fresh perspective to the industry, and to pave the way for others like herself.

Fawn's experiences as a black woman in a predominantly male industry were not always easy. She encountered scepticism, doubt, and outright racism. Some questioned whether she possessed the knowledge, expertise, or passion required to succeed in the whiskey industry. Some people questioned her ability to create a premium whiskey brand simply because she was a woman. But Fawn didn't let their doubts stop her. She worked harder, learned more, and proved them incorrect.

One of the most significant obstacles Fawn encountered was a lack of access to capital. As a black woman, she lacked the same connections, networks, and funding opportunities as her male counterparts. But Fawn was determined to find a solution. She worked tirelessly to establish relationships, secure funding, and develop a brand that would stand out in a competitive market.

Fawn's determination, passion, and refusal to be stymied by obstacles ultimately paid off. Uncle Nearest Premium Whiskey debuted to critical acclaim, with whiskey enthusiasts and industry insiders praising its smooth, rich flavour and historical significance. The brand quickly developed a devoted following, with fans from all over the world seeking out Fawn's whiskey.

As Fawn reflected on her journey, she realised that breaking down barriers was about more than just her own success. It was about paving the way for others, forging a path for those who followed her. It was about demonstrating to the world that a black woman could succeed in a male-dominated industry, that she could launch a premium whiskey brand, and make a difference.

Fawn's story demonstrates that obstacles are not insurmountable, that challenges can be overcome, and that determination, passion, and hard work can lead to success. It demonstrates the power of entrepreneurship, innovation, and the power of pursuing one's dreams, no matter how impossible they may appear.

Fawn Weaver's journey is a beacon of hope, demonstrating what we can accomplish when we combine our passions, talents, and values. It serves as a reminder that we all have the ability to break down barriers, shatter glass ceilings, and change the world.

CHAPTER 5

THE WHISKEY QUEEN

Fawn Weaver's rise to celebrity was nothing short of meteoric. From the launch of Uncle Nearest Premium Whiskey to her numerous awards, recognition, and media appearances, Fawn's star has grown brighter with each passing day. She was hailed as a trailblazer, pioneer, and game changer in the whiskey industry, and her name came to represent excellence, innovation, and passion.

Fawn's numerous awards and accolades for Uncle Nearest Premium Whiskey were one of the first signs of her rising fame. The brand received top honours at prestigious spirits competitions such as the San Francisco World Spirits Competition, the International Whiskey Competition, and the Whiskey Awards. Fawn's whiskey was lauded for its rich, smooth flavour, historical significance, and dedication to quality and craftsmanship.

Fawn's brand gained recognition, and she began to receive media attention from leading publications and outlets. She has been featured in Forbes, Entrepreneur, and Inc. magazines, as well as on television shows, podcasts, and radio programs such as NPR, CNN, and Bloomberg. Fawn's story was inspiring; her enthusiasm was contagious, and her knowledge was unparalleled.

Fawn's media appearances were always met with high praise. She was a natural in front of the camera, with a warm smile, quick wit, and a thorough understanding of whiskey. Her humility, kindness, and generosity endeared her to audiences, and her story of perseverance, determination, and success inspired countless people.

One of Fawn's media highlights was her appearance on the cover of Whiskey Advocate magazine. The publication, widely regarded as the authority on whiskey, dubbed Fawn the Whiskey Queen, and her cover story reflected her influence on the industry. The article was a beautiful tribute to Fawn's passion, dedication, and commitment to excellence.

Fawn's rise to fame resulted in numerous speaking engagements and appearances at whiskey festivals and events. She was a popular speaker, known for her motivational talks, whiskey expertise, and contagious enthusiasm. Fawn's appearances were always greeted with standing ovations, and her fans would frequently queue for hours to meet her, sample her whiskey, and hear her story.

As Fawn's fame grew, she began to receive recognition at the highest levels. She was invited to the White House for a whiskey tasting event, and the Tennessee State Legislature recognized her contributions to the state's whiskey industry. Fawn's awards and recognition reflected her hard work, dedication, and enthusiasm for whiskey.

Fawn Weaver's rise to fame demonstrated the power of entrepreneurship, innovation, and pursuing one's dreams. She was a true pioneer, trailblazer, and game changer in the whiskey industry, and her legacy will continue to inspire future generations.

CHAPTER 6

RACISM AND SEXISM WITHIN THE INDUSTRY

Fawn Weaver's journey in the whiskey industry was not without challenges. As a black woman, she encountered racism and sexism at every turn, from investors' scepticism to the condescension of industry insiders. However, Fawn was not deterred by obstacles. She was motivated by a love of whiskey, a desire to succeed, and a refusal to be limited by the status quo.

Fawn first encountered racism in the industry while looking for funding for her brand. She met with a number of investors, but many of them questioned her ability to succeed in the whiskey industry. They frequently made comments about her lack of experience, knowledge, and connections. But Fawn knew that these remarks were not about her abilities, but about her race and gender.

Fawn approached these encounters with courage and determination. She conducted research, honed her pitch, and practised her responses to common objections. She also sought out mentors and advisors who could guide her through the industry and provide advice on how to overcome the challenges she faced.

Another encounter with racism in the industry occurred when Fawn was attempting to secure distribution for her brand. She met with a number of distributors, but most of them were hesitant to work with her. They would frequently comment on the lack of demand for whiskey from a black-owned brand, or the lack of interest in whiskey from a female entrepreneur. However, Fawn recognized that these comments were about the distributors' biases and prejudices, not the market itself.

Fawn addressed these encounters through creativity and innovation. She devised a unique distribution strategy that centred on cultivating relationships with independent retailers and restaurateurs. She also collaborated with other black-owned businesses to form a group that could negotiate better terms with distributors.

Fawn's encounters with sexism in the industry were equally challenging. She encountered condescension and scepticism from male industry insiders who did not believe a woman could create a premium whiskey brand. They frequently made comments about her lack of knowledge, experience, and physical strength. But Fawn knew the comments were about her gender, not her abilities.

Fawn handled the encounters with confidence and assertiveness. She educated herself on all aspects of the whiskey industry, from distillation to marketing. She also built a solid network of female mentors and advisors who could offer advice and support.

One of Fawn's most memorable encounters with sexism in the industry occurred when she was attempting to secure a spot at a prestigious whiskey festival. The festival organisers were hesitant to include her brand, citing concerns about the whiskey's quality and a lack of interest in whiskey from a female entrepreneur. But Fawn knew that her concerns were not about her whiskey, but about her gender.

Fawn approached this encounter with determination and perseverance. She entered her whiskey into numerous spirits competitions, where it won first place and received critical acclaim. She also established a strong social media presence, where she could interact with her followers and promote her brand.

Fawn Weaver's encounters with racism and sexism in the whiskey industry demonstrated her courage, determination, and refusal to be held back by adversity. She responded to these encounters with creativity, innovation, and a commitment to excellence, establishing herself as an industry leader.

CHAPTER 7

CRITICISM AND BACKLASH

Fawn Weaver's rise to fame was not without challenges. As a black woman in a male-dominated industry, she received criticism and backlash from both the general public and industry peers. Some questioned her qualifications, expertise, and ability to launch a premium whiskey brand. Some criticised her marketing strategy, branding, and business model. But Fawn was undeterred by criticism. She was motivated by a love of whiskey, a desire to succeed, and a refusal to be stifled by negativity.

One of the first criticisms Fawn received came from industry insiders who questioned her lack of experience in the whiskey industry. They frequently referred to her as a "novice" or "newbie" who knew nothing about whiskey.

But Fawn knew that these remarks were not about her abilities, but about her gender and race. She responded to these criticisms by educating herself on all aspects of the whiskey industry, from distillation to marketing. She also built an extensive network of mentors and advisors who could offer advice and support.

Another criticism Fawn received was from whiskey enthusiasts, who questioned the quality of her whiskey. They would frequently comment on the flavour profile, ageing process, and ingredients used. But Fawn knew the comments weren't about the whiskey; they were about her brand and reputation.

She responded to these criticisms by submitting her whiskey to numerous spirits competitions, where it won first place and received critical acclaim. She also established a strong social media presence, where she could interact with her followers and promote her brand.

Fawn also received criticism from industry colleagues who felt threatened by her success. They would frequently comment on her being "lucky" or "privileged" to have achieved such success in such a short period of time. But Fawn knew the comments were about their own insecurities and fears, not her success. She responded to these criticisms by remaining focused on her goals, true to her vision, and committed to her values.

One of the most serious criticisms Fawn received came from a prominent whiskey critic who wrote a harsh review of her whiskey. The critic questioned the whiskey's quality, ingredients, and ageing process. But Fawn understood that this review was about the critic's own biases and prejudices, not the whiskey itself. She handled the criticism by remaining calm, professional, and focused on her goals. She also had a strong reaction to the criticism, which she shared on social media and with her fans.

Fawn Weaver's ability to handle criticism and backlash from the public and industry peers demonstrated her strength, resilience, and determination. She handled the criticisms with grace, humility, and a dedication to excellence. She came out of these challenges stronger, wiser, and more confident than ever before.

Fawn's story serves as a reminder that criticism and backlash are unavoidable components of success. They are evidence that we are doing something right, pushing boundaries, and making a difference. However, how we respond to these criticisms is what really matters. Do we let them hold us back, or do we see them as a chance to grow, learn, and improve?

Fawn's response to criticism and backlash reflected her character, values, and vision. She remained true to herself, true to her brand, and committed to her goals. She emerged from these challenges as a leader, role model, and true pioneer in the whiskey industry.

CHAPTER 8

PERSONAL STRUGGLES

Fawn Weaver's path to success was not without personal struggles. Behind the scenes of her whiskey empire, Fawn struggled with health issues, relationship problems, and personal doubts that threatened to derail her ambitions. But Fawn was not someone to give up easily. She was motivated by a love of whiskey, a desire to succeed, and a refusal to let her personal issues hold her back.

One of Fawn's most difficult personal struggles was her battle with anxiety and depression. As a black woman in a male-dominated industry, Fawn frequently felt like she was bearing the weight of the world on her shoulders. She'd frequently wake up in the middle of the night, her mind racing with feelings of failure, rejection, and inadequacy. But Fawn understood that she couldn't let her anxiety and depression define her. She went to therapy, practised self-care, and surrounded herself with a supportive group of friends and family.

Fawn's health problems were another personal challenge she faced. As a whiskey entrepreneur, Fawn was always on the move, attending events, meetings, and tastings. She frequently neglected her own health, skipping meals and sacrificing sleep. But Fawn knew she couldn't keep up this pace. She started prioritising her health, eating nutritious foods, exercising regularly, and getting enough sleep. She also learned to decline events and commitments that could jeopardise her health.

Fawn's relationship issues were another personal challenge she encountered. As a successful entrepreneur, Fawn received a lot of attention, both positive and negative. She would frequently find herself in relationships that were more about the whiskey brand than about her as a person. But Fawn knew she deserved more. She started to prioritise her own needs, desires, and happiness. She surrounded herself with people who loved and supported her, and she learned how to set boundaries and prioritise her personal relationships.

Despite her personal struggles, Fawn remained dedicated to her whiskey brand. She put her heart and soul into every bottle, label, and marketing campaign. She was motivated by a love of whiskey, a desire to succeed, and a refusal to let her personal issues hold her back.

Fawn's personal struggles taught her important lessons in resilience, perseverance, and self-care. She realised that success is more than just achieving your goals; it is also about taking care of yourself along the way. She learned that it's okay to ask for assistance, seek support, and prioritise your own needs. And she realised that even in the darkest of times, there is always hope and a way forward.

Fawn Weaver's personal struggles demonstrated her strength, courage, and resilience. She confronted her challenges head on, sought assistance and support, and emerged stronger, wiser, and more confident than ever before. Her story reminds us that success is more than just achieving your goals; it's also about taking care of yourself along the way.

Fawn's whiskey brand became a representation of her personal struggles and triumphs. Every bottle, label, and marketing campaign demonstrated her courage, resilience, and determination. Her whiskey brand was more than just a business; it reflected her own personal journey, struggles, and triumphs.

Fawn's story reminds us that we are not alone in our personal struggles. We all face challenges, uncertainties, and fears. However, how we respond to these challenges is what matters most. Do we let them hold us back, or do we see them as a chance to grow, learn, and overcome?

CHAPTER 9

GIVING BACK

Fawn Weaver's rise to fame was driven not only by her whiskey brand, but also by her desire to make a difference in her community. As a black woman in a male-dominated industry, Fawn understood her responsibility to give back, pay it forward, and make a difference. So she established the Uncle Nearest Foundation, a non-profit organisation dedicated to assisting African American entrepreneurs, farmers, and distillers.

The Uncle Nearest Foundation was more than just a philanthropic endeavour; it was Fawn's passion project. She had always been motivated by a desire to help others, empower her community, and provide opportunities for those who had been marginalised and overlooked. Fawn established the foundation to provide scholarships, mentorship, and resources to African American entrepreneurs interested in starting their own whiskey businesses.

One of the most important initiatives of the Uncle Nearest Foundation was its scholarship program. Fawn recognized that one of the most significant barriers to entry for African American entrepreneurs was access to capital. As a result, she established a scholarship program to support students pursuing degrees in fields related to the whiskey industry. The program was a huge success, with dozens of students receiving scholarships and eventually starting their own businesses.

The Uncle Nearest Foundation also launched a mentorship program. Fawn understood that mentorship was critical to success, particularly for African American entrepreneurs who frequently lacked access to networks and resources.
As a result, she established a mentorship program that connected African American

entrepreneurs with experienced mentors in the whiskey industry. The program was a huge success, with many entrepreneurs going on to start and run their own businesses with great success.

Fawn's charitable efforts were not overlooked. She was recognized by her community, industry, and the media for her tireless efforts and commitment to giving back. She received numerous awards and honours, including the prestigious Entrepreneur of the Year award.

However, Fawn's philanthropic efforts were not solely about recognition or awards. They were about making an impact, creating opportunities, and empowering her community. And this is exactly what she did. Fawn established an enduring legacy through the Uncle Nearest Foundation, inspiring and empowering future generations.

Fawn's story reminds us that success is more than just achieving our goals; it's also about giving back to our community. It is about leveraging our resources, talents, and platforms to make a difference. And it is about providing opportunities for others, particularly those who have been marginalised and overlooked.

Fawn Weaver's philanthropic efforts reflected her character, values, and dedication to giving back. She was a true leader, entrepreneur, and philanthropist. Her legacy would continue to inspire and empower future generations.

Fawn's whiskey brand became a symbol of her philanthropic efforts, a reminder of the difference she wished to make in her community. Every bottle, label, and marketing campaign demonstrated her dedication to giving back, empowering her community, and providing opportunities for others.

Fawn's story serves as a reminder that we all have the ability to make a difference, give back, and create opportunities for other people. We all have the ability to use our resources, talents, and platforms to empower our communities and make a positive difference in the world. And it is up to us to use that power wisely, to make a difference, and to leave a legacy that will last beyond us.

CHAPTER 10

CREATING A LASTING LEGACY

Fawn Weaver's contributions to the whiskey industry were nothing short of revolutionary. She was a trailblazer, innovator, and game changer. She broke down barriers, shattered glass ceilings, and set the example for others to follow in her footsteps. Throughout it all, she remained humble, kind, and dedicated to her craft.

Fawn's impact on the whiskey industry was far-reaching. She influenced a new generation of whiskey enthusiasts, encouraged women and minorities to enter the industry, and pushed the limits of what was possible with whiskey. She was a true innovator, entrepreneur, and leader.

One of the most significant contributions Fawn made to the whiskey industry was her commitment to diversity and inclusion. She was an outspoken supporter of women and minorities in the industry, and she worked tirelessly to create opportunities for them. She was a mentor, role model, and source of inspiration for many people looking to break into the industry.

Fawn's commitment to diversity and inclusion was more than just doing the right thing; it was about making the industry better for everyone. She understood that the whiskey industry thrived when it was diverse, inclusive, and reflective of the world around us. She worked tirelessly to make her vision a reality.

Fawn's influence on the whiskey industry was also felt through her innovative approach to whiskey production. She was a true artist, a true craftsman, and an absolute master of her trade. She pushed the boundaries of whiskey, experimenting with new flavours and techniques to create truly unique and exceptional whiskeys.

Fawn's whiskeys were about more than just the liquid in the bottle; they were about the experience, emotion, and connection they evoked. They were about bringing people together, making memories, and making each moment special. They were about celebrating whiskey's beauty, complexity, and diversity.

As Fawn looked ahead, she had hopes for the industry she loved. She hoped it would continue to evolve, innovate, and push the envelope of what was possible. She hoped it would continue to be a place where people could gather, share their passions, and create something truly unique.

Fawn also hoped that the industry would continue to value diversity and inclusion. She hoped that it would continue to provide opportunities for women and minorities while also celebrating the unique perspectives and experiences that they brought to the table. She hoped it would remain a place where everyone felt welcomed, valued, and empowered to succeed.

Finally, Fawn Weaver's legacy extended beyond her whiskey brand, business, or industry. It was about how she affected those around her, the connections she made, and the memories she created. It was about how she made people feel, how she inspired and empowered them.

Fawn's legacy demonstrated the power of passion, purpose, and perseverance. It was a reminder that we all have the ability to make a difference, create something truly unique, and leave a lasting legacy. And it was a challenge to us all to use that power wisely, to make a positive difference in the world, and to build a better future for everyone.

Fawn's story serves as a reminder that we all have the ability to create something truly unique, make a difference, and leave a lasting impact. We each have the ability to inspire, empower, and connect with others. And we all have the ability to shape a better future for everyone.

CONCLUSION

The Fawn Weaver Story.

As we reflect on Fawn's life, accomplishments, and lessons learned, we are reminded of the importance of passion, purpose, and perseverance. Fawn's story demonstrates that with hard work, determination, and a willingness to take risks, we can accomplish whatever we set our minds to.

Fawn's journey began with a simple desire for whiskey. She was captivated by the complexity, nuance, and beauty of this ancient spirit. But as she learned more about whiskey, she realised that it was more than just the liquid in the bottle. She saw an industry dominated by men, slow to evolve, and in need of a new perspective.

Fawn set out to make a difference. She created her own whiskey brand, Uncle Nearest, and put her heart and soul into each bottle. She travelled the world, learning from master distillers, trying out new flavours, and honing her craft. She worked tirelessly to promote her brand, establish a community of whiskey enthusiasts, and spark a movement.

But Fawn's impact extended far beyond her brand. She influenced a new generation of whiskey enthusiasts, encouraged women and minorities to enter the industry, and pushed the limits of what was possible with whiskey. She was a true innovator, entrepreneur, and leader.

As we reflect on Fawn's accomplishments, we are reminded of the value of taking risks, being bold, and fearless. Fawn's journey was not without obstacles, setbacks, and failures. Despite these obstacles, she never gave up. She persevered, adapted, and overcame.

Fawn's story demonstrates the power of community, collaboration, and connection. She created a brand that focused on the people around her rather than just herself. She cultivated a community of whiskey enthusiasts who shared her enthusiasm, values, and vision. She worked tirelessly to promote her brand, build relationships, and provide opportunities for others.

As we look ahead, we are reminded of the lessons Fawn has learned along the way. We are reminded how important it is to stay true to ourselves, our values, and our vision. We are reminded of the value of taking risks, being bold, and fearless. And we're reminded of the value of community, collaboration, and connection.

Fawn's story reminds us that we all have the ability to make a difference, create something truly unique, and leave a lasting legacy. We each have the ability to inspire, empower, and connect with others. And we all have the ability to shape a better future for everyone.

Finally, Fawn Weaver's story exemplifies the strength of the human spirit. It serves as a reminder that we all have the potential to achieve greatness, make a difference, and leave a lasting legacy. And it is a challenge to each of us to use our talents, passions, and values to make the world a better place for everyone.

Fawn's legacy will live on through her brand, community, and the countless lives she has impacted. She will be regarded as a true pioneer, trailblazer, and game changer in the whiskey industry. She will be remembered as a true inspiration, role model, and leader.

As we conclude this chapter in Fawn Weaver's story, we are left with feelings of awe, admiration, and gratitude. We are left wondering about the impact that a single person can have on the world. And we are left with a sense of hope for the future, knowing that people like Fawn are out there making a difference, creating something truly unique, and leaving a lasting legacy.

Made in the USA
Las Vegas, NV
26 April 2025

21402026R00036